Questions and Answers: Countries

Canada

by Nathan Olson

Consultant:
Barry Ferguson
Professor of History, University of Manitoba
Winnipeg, Manitoba, Canada

Capstone press

Mankato, Minnesota

Fact Finders is published by Capstone Press
151 Good Counsel Drive, P.O. Box 669, Mankato, Minnesota 56002
www.capstonepress.com

Library of Congress Cataloging-in-Publication Data
Olson, Nathan.
  Canada / by Nathan Olson.
    p. cm.—(Fact finders. Questions and answers. Countries)
  Includes bibliographical references and index.
  Contents: Where is Canada?—When did Canada become a country?—What type of
government does Canada have?—What kind of housing does Canada have?—What are
Canada's forms of transportation?—What are Canada's major industries?—What is school
like in Canada?—What are Canada's favorite sports and games?—What are the traditional
art forms in Canada?—What major holidays do people in Canada celebrate?—What are the
traditional foods of Canada?—What is family life like in Canada?—Canada fast facts—
Money and flag—Learn to speak French.
  ISBN 0-7368-2686-6 (hardcover)
  1. Canada—Juvenile literature. I. Title. II. Series.
F1008.2.O46 2005
971—dc22   2003025517

Editorial Credits
Christine Peterson, editor; Kia Adams, series designer; Jennifer Bergstrom, book designer;
  maps.com, map illustrator; Wanda Winch, photo researcher; Scott Thoms, photo editor;
  Eric Kudalis, product planning editor

Photo Credits
AP/Wide World Photos/Canadian Press/Ron Poling, 7; Bruce Coleman Inc./John Elk III,
25; Canadian Library of Parliament/Stephen Fenn, 8–9; Capstone Press Archives, 29 (top);
Corbis/AFP, 21; Corbis/Alain Le Garsmeur, 11; Corbis/Annie Griffiths Belt, 16–17;
Corbis/Gunter Marx Photography, 13; Corbis/Paul A. Souders, 15; Corbis/Ron Watts, cover
(foreground); Corbis/Staffan Widstrand, 12; Corel, 1; Getty Images Inc./Al Bello, 18–19;
Photodisc/Amanda Clement, cover (background); Stockhaus Limited, 29 (bottom); Tom
Stack & Associates Inc./Thomas Kitchin, 4; TRIP/N. Price, 16; Wolfgang Kaehler, 23, 27

Artistic Effects
Corel, 20 (soapstone bear); Photodisc/Don Tremain, 18 (hockey puck); Photodisc/Siede
Preis, 6 (maple leaf)

1 2 3 4 5 6 09 08 07 06 05 04

Table of Contents

Features

Where is Canada?

Canada is a large country that borders the northern United States. Canada's land size makes it the second largest country in the world after Russia.

Many landforms cover Canada. The St. Lawrence River flows northeast from the Great Lakes into the Atlantic Ocean. Farmland covers the southeast.

The St. Lawrence River carries more goods in Canada than any other river in the country. ➤

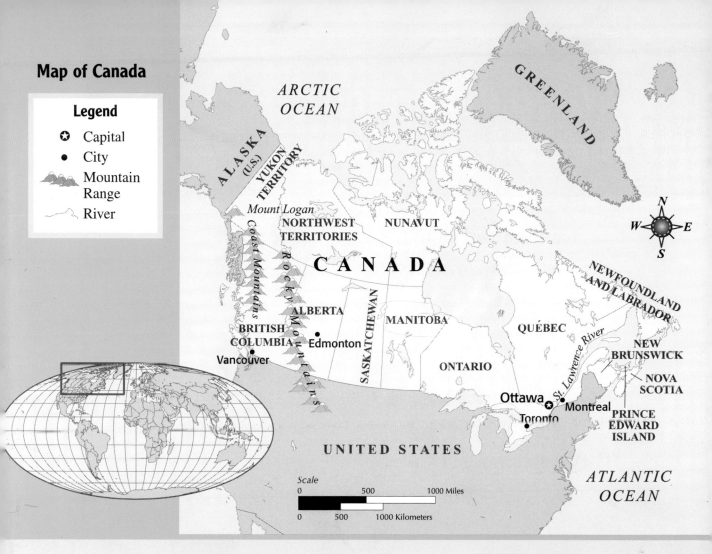

Map of Canada

Legend

✪	Capital
●	City
⛰	Mountain Range
∼	River

ARCTIC OCEAN

GREENLAND

ALASKA (U.S.)

YUKON TERRITORY

Mount Logan

NORTHWEST TERRITORIES

NUNAVUT

CANADA

Coast Mountains

Rocky Mountains

ALBERTA

BRITISH COLUMBIA

Edmonton

Vancouver

SASKATCHEWAN

MANITOBA

ONTARIO

QUÉBEC

NEWFOUNDLAND AND LABRADOR

St. Lawrence River

NEW BRUNSWICK

NOVA SCOTIA

Ottawa ✪ Montreal

Toronto

PRINCE EDWARD ISLAND

UNITED STATES

ATLANTIC OCEAN

N W E S

Scale
0   500   1000 Miles
0   500   1000 Kilometers

Canada is home to a large wilderness area. Lakes and forests cover the land. To the north lies the Arctic Ocean. Arctic winds and snow shape this land. Plains roll west across Canada to the Rocky and Coast Mountains.

When did Canada become a country?

The **Dominion** of Canada was formed on July 1, 1867. On that day, leaders signed the British North American Act. Since 1763, Great Britain had ruled Canada. At that time, the land was divided into areas called **provinces**.

In 1867, three provinces joined together. They became the Dominion of Canada. People soon moved to new parts of the country. They formed new provinces.

Fact!

In 1965, Canadians agreed on a new flag with a red maple leaf. The 11-point maple leaf is Canada's national symbol.

In 1982, Great Britain's Queen Elizabeth II signed the Canada and Constitution Acts.

Over time, Canada grew more independent from Great Britain. In 1982, Canada and Great Britain signed the Canada and Constitution Acts. These acts allowed Canada to make its own laws.

What type of government does Canada have?

Canada's government is a **constitutional monarchy**. In this system, the king or queen of Great Britain is the head of state. The governor general represents the king or queen in Canada.

Canada's **parliament** makes laws. The parliament has two parts, the Senate and the House of Commons. These groups meet in the capital city of Ottawa.

Fact!

The king or queen of Great Britain does not have any real power in Canada. The king or queen is part of the government to honor Canada's past.

Canada's House of Commons, above, has 301 members. The Senate has 105 members.

Canada's **prime minister** leads the government. The prime minister and governor general both sign laws. The governor general signs the law to show that the king or queen also agrees with it.

What kind of housing does Canada have?

Most Canadians live in or near cities. Most families live in houses with two to four bedrooms. In Canada's largest cities, people often live in smaller houses or apartments. Some people live in houses in Canada's large wilderness areas.

Where do people in Canada live?

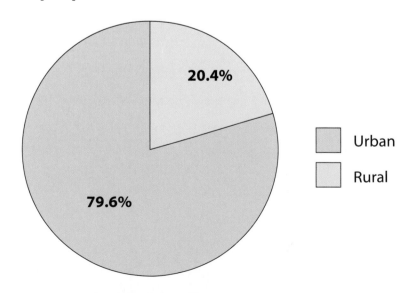

20.4%

79.6%

Urban

Rural

Snow piles up against a house in Canada's Nunavut province.

Inuit (IN-oo-it) people live in Canada's far north. They were among Canada's first people. Most Inuit live in small houses. Some Inuit move from place to place. They live in tents made from animal skins.

What are Canada's forms of transportation?

Canadians use many forms of transportation. Many people own cars. Southern Canada has a good road system. People in large cities often ride buses.

Airplanes are important to Canadians. Airplanes take most goods and people across the country. In the past, railroads carried most goods across Canada.

In Canada's far north, many people use snowmobiles to carry goods and supplies. ▶

The Trans Canada is the world's largest highway. It stretches east and west across Canada for 4,860 miles (7,821 kilometers).

In the far north, people travel across the snowy land in many ways. Some people use skis and snowmobiles. Others use dogsleds. In the summer, people also use boats and canoes on lakes and rivers.

What is school like in Canada?

Canadian schools are like schools in the United States. Most children in Canada go to public school. Some families pay to send their children to private schools.

Canadian students study many subjects. They study math, social studies, and science. Students learn English and French. Many Canadians speak both languages.

Classrooms in Canada look like those in U.S. schools. ➤

Some Canadian students go to private schools.

Each province makes its own rules for schools. Most children start school when they are 5 years old. They must go to school until they are 15 or 16 years old. Grade school lasts from kindergarten through eighth grade. Most students then go to high school. Many students also go to college.

What are Canada's favorite sports and games?

Ice hockey is Canada's most popular sport. Canadians invented this game in the late 1800s. Canadians enjoy watching and playing ice hockey year-round.

Lacrosse is Canada's official sport. Canada's native people first played this game. Lacrosse players carry a long stick with a net on the end. They pass a ball using this stick.

Fact!

Canadian Wayne Gretzky is considered the greatest hockey player of all time. While he played pro hockey, Gretzky scored a record 2,857 points. He retired in 1999.

In 2002, the Canadian men's hockey team won the gold medal at the Winter Olympics in Salt Lake City, Utah.

People in Canada enjoy many other sports. Curling is a popular game. In curling, players slide large smooth stones over ice toward a target. Children in Canada also enjoy basketball, soccer, and ice-skating.

What are the traditional art forms in Canada?

Canadians enjoy many forms of art. Museums show art from Canada and around the world. Inuit stone carvings are on display in many museums.

Canada is home to many writers. Their works are world famous. Lucy Maud Montgomery is a popular Canadian writer. Her 1909 book, *Anne of Green Gables*, still sells thousands of copies each year.

Fact!

Inuit art dates back to 600 BC. The Inuit carved wood, bone, and ivory into animals, masks, and other figures.

Inuit artists carefully carve stone into animal sculptures.

Canadians also enjoy different types of music, dance, and theater. Many of Canada's large cities have their own orchestras, ballet companies, and operas. Montreal's Cirque du Soleil is a world-famous circus.

What major holidays do people in Canada celebrate?

People in Canada celebrate Canada Day on July 1. This holiday marks the day when three provinces formed one country. People celebrate this holiday with parties, music, and fireworks.

Canadians have many other holidays. People celebrate Labor Day in September. This holiday honors Canadian workers. Remembrance Day is held on November 11. On this day, people remember the men and women who fought in wars for Canada.

What other holidays do people in Canada celebrate?

Boxing Day
Thanksgiving (October)
Victoria Day

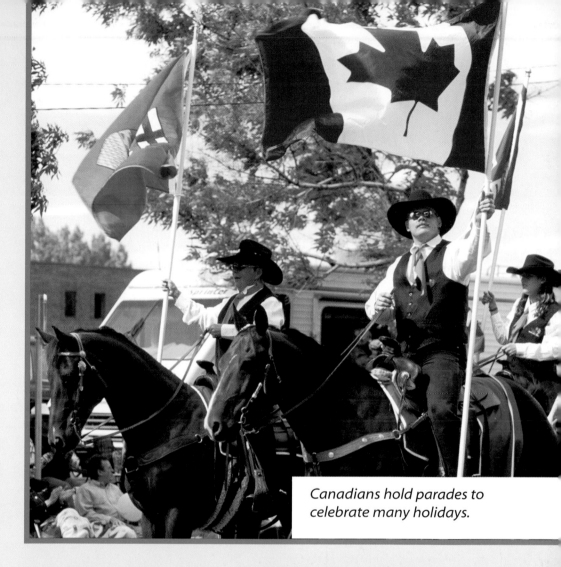

Canadians hold parades to celebrate many holidays.

Many Canadians also celebrate religious holidays. In March or April, families gather for Easter. On December 25, Canadians celebrate Christmas.

What are the traditional foods of Canada?

Canadians enjoy many foods. They eat meat, vegetables, and grains from Canada's farms. People living near the coasts enjoy fish and other seafood. Some people hunt deer, moose, and other wild animals for food. Most of the world's maple syrup comes from Canada.

Fact!

People in eastern Canada pour hot maple syrup over fresh snow. The snow cools the syrup and a chewy candy forms.

In Canada's coastal cities, people shop for fresh fish and seafood.

Some provinces have their own special foods. In Québec, people eat a meat pie called a *tourtière*. People in British Columbia pick berries to make jams and jellies.

What is family life like in Canada?

Canadian families are smaller than they were 25 years ago. Most families have only one or two children. Canadian adults are also waiting longer to have children.

Higher living costs are also changing the Canadian family. In most families, both parents need to work outside the home.

What are the ethnic backgrounds of people in Canada?

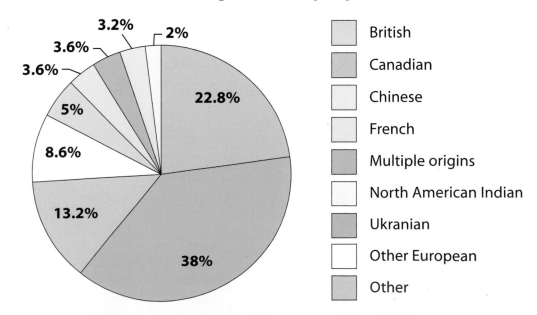

	British
	Canadian
	Chinese
	French
	Multiple origins
	North American Indian
	Ukranian
	Other European
	Other

3.2% 2% 3.6% 3.6% 5% 8.6% 13.2% 22.8% 38%

Canadian families enjoy ice-skating and many other outdoor activities together.

In some families, grandparents and other members moved to Canada from different countries. Many families carry on **customs** from these countries. These families help to make Canada a unique country.

Canada Fast Facts

Official name:

Dominion of Canada

Land area:

3,855,081 square miles
(9,984,670 square kilometers)

**Average annual
precipitation (Ottawa):**

35 inches (89 centimeters)

**Average
January temperature
(Ottawa):**

12 degrees Fahrenheit
(minus 11 degrees Celsius)

**Average
July temperature (Ottawa):**

69 degrees Fahrenheit
(21 degrees Celsius)

Population:

32,207,113 people

Capital city:

Ottawa

Languages:

English and French

Natural resources:

coal, forests, iron ore, oil

Religions:

Roman Catholic	46%
Protestant	36%
Other	18%

Money and Flag

Money:

*Canada's money is the Canadian dollar. In 2004,
1 U.S. dollar equaled 1.28 Canadian dollars.*

Flag:

*In 1965, Canadians chose a new flag for their country. The Canadian flag is
red and white with an 11-point maple leaf in the center. Red and white are
Canada's national colors.*

29

Learn to Speak French

Many people in Canada speak both English and French. Children in Canada learn both languages. Learn to speak some French using the words below.

English	French	Pronunciation
good-bye	au revouir	(oh ruh-VWAH)
good morning	bonjour	(bohn-JOOR)
sorry	désolé	(day-zoh-LAY)
please	s´il vous plaît	(SEEL VOO PLAY)
thank you	merci	(mare-SEE)
yes	oui	(WEE)
no	non	(NOHN)

Glossary

constitutional monarchy (kon-sti-TOO-shuhn-uhl MON-ar-kee)—a system of government in which the monarch's powers are limited

custom (KUHSS-tuhm)—a tradition in a culture or society

dominion (duh-MIN-yuhn)—a large area of land controlled by a single ruler or government

parliament (PAR-luh-muhnt)—the group of people who have been elected to make laws in some countries

prime minister (PRIME MIN-uh-stur)—the person in charge of a government in some countries

province (PROV-uhnss)—a district or a region of some countries; Canada is divided into provinces.

Internet Sites

FactHound offers a safe, fun way to find Internet sites related to this book. All of the sites on FactHound have been researched by our staff.

Here's how:
1. Visit *www.facthound.com*
2. Type in this special code **0736826866** for age-appropriate sites. Or enter a search word related to this book for a more general search.
3. Click on the **Fetch It** button.

FactHound will fetch the best sites for you!

Read More

Gray, Shirley W. *Canada.* First Reports. Minneapolis: Compass Point Books, 2000.

McCarthy, Pat. *Canada.* Top Ten Countries of Recent Immigrants. Berkeley Heights, NJ: MyReportLinks.com Books, 2004.

Olson, Kay Melchisedech. *Canada.* Many Cultures, One World. Mankato, Minn.: Blue Earth Books, 2004.

Quigley, Mary. *Canada.* A Visit To. Chicago: Heinemann, 2003.

Index